D1220700

THIS NOTEBOOK
BELOGS TO :

____